MORE TRIOS for Trumpets

21 Distinctive Arrangements of Famous Music

JOHN CACAVAS

D1302332

ISBN 0-7390-2328-4

Washington Post

John Philip Sousa
Arr. by John Cacavas

Trumpet Voluntary

Jeremiah Clarke
Arr. by John Cacavas

Ode to Joy

Beethoven
Arr. by John Cacavas

Fanfare from William Tell Overture

Rossini
Arr. by John Cacavas

America
("God Save the Queen")

Carey
Arr. by John Cacavas

The Great Gate of Kiev
(from *Pictures at an Exhibition*)

Mussorgsky
Arr. by John Cacavas

Maple Leaf Rag

Joplin
Arr. by John Cacavas

La Cucaracha

Traditional Mexican Folk Song
Arr. by John Cacavas

British Grenadiers

Traditional
Arr. by John Cacavas

Tarantella

Italian Folk Dance
Arr. by John Cacavas

Angels We Have Heard on High

Traditional Christmas Carol
Arr. by John Cacavas

Soldier's Chorus
(from the Opera *Faust*)

Gounod
Arr. by John Cacavas

(I'm A) Yankee Doodle Dandy

George M. Cohan
Arr. by John Cacavas

The Minstrel Boy

Irish Air
Arr. by John Cacavas

Give My Regards to Broadway

George M. Cohan
Arr. by John Cacavas

Little Brown Jug

Winner
Arr. by John Cacavas

Fanfares

By John Cacavas

Oh! Susanna

Foster
Arr. by John Cacavas

O Little Town of Bethlehem

Redner
Arr. by John Cacavas

Jolly Old St. Nicholas

Traditional
Arr. by John Cacavas

She Wore a Yellow Ribbon

Traditional
Arr. by John Cacavas